the Fir Brothers

Genesis 4:1–15 for children

Written by Joan E. Curren
Illustrated by Allan Eitzen

CONCORDIA PUBLISHING HOUSE • SAINT LOUIS

Cain was born to Adam and Eve.
They rocked him in his cradle.
Then as Cain grew, they wanted two.
Soon came brother Abel.

They laughed and played, sang silly songs,
Got into trouble too.
Then Eve would scold her precious sons
Just like our mothers do.

"I love the frisky, woolly lambs.
Just watch them jump and play,"
Laughed Abel as they licked his hand.
"I'll have some sheep someday."

"That's good!" crowed Cain and clapped his hands.
"Their wool will keep us warm.
Then I will plant and gather all
Our food from my own farm."

When they were grown, then Abel said,
"The best of lambs I'll give
In sacrifice with love to God
As long as I shall live."

Cain said, "I guess that I should too.
I'd really rather not.
Instead I'll give some grain and fruit
That I won't miss a lot."

Then God looked deep into their hearts.
In Abel's He saw love.
Cain's heart was hard—and selfish too—
No respect for God above.

So God accepted Abel's gift,
But Cain's gift He refused.
Cain hung his head and kicked the dirt
And scowled. He was confused.

"Why are you mad and scowling so?
You could be glad," God said.
"You will be when you do what's right
And give your best instead."

"Now sin is like a monster huge
That's crouching by the door."
Then God said, "You can master it.
I'll help you win that war."

Cain searched for Abel. Then he said,
"Out to the field let's go."
And when they got there, Cain attacked—
Killed Abel with a blow.

Then God asked Cain, "Where's Abel now?"
Cain lied, "I do not know.
Am I my brother's keeper, Lord?"
God said, "You'll have much woe—

"Because I know the truth. You killed
Your brother by your hand.
Now you will have no home or friends.
You'll wander through the land."

"This punishment I cannot bear.
I'll be alone!" cried Cain.
"Without *You*, God, and with no home,
By strangers I'll be slain!"

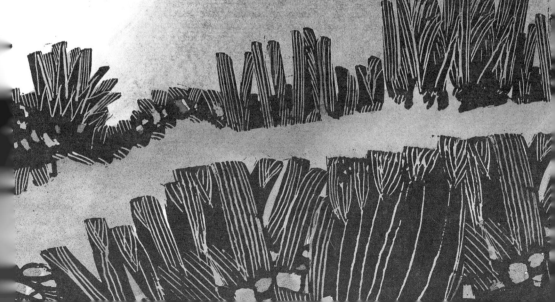

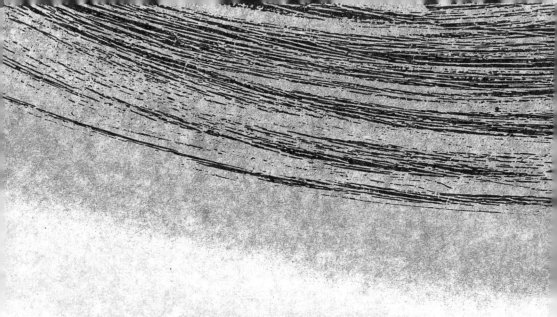

"You won't be killed." God soothed Cain's fear.
"Although your sin is great,
You'll wear My mark of mercy, Cain—
Protection against hate."

Though Cain had sinned, God loved him still.
The killing was not right.
But God, through Jesus, *does* forgive
And loves us day and night.

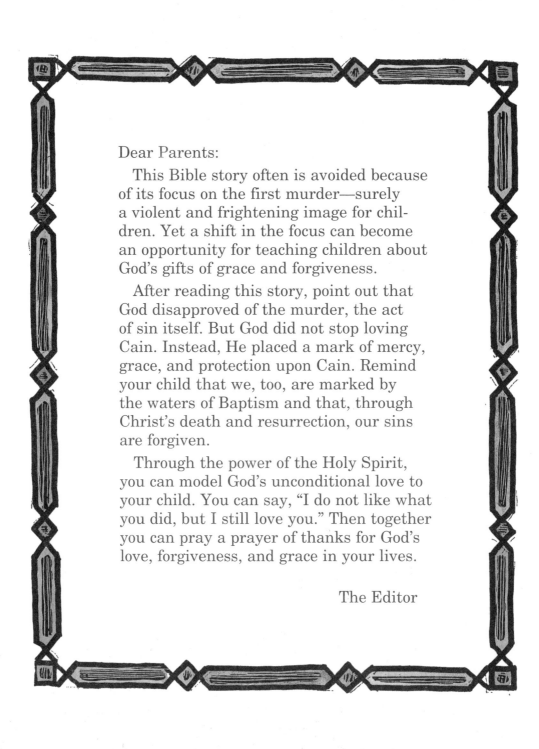

Dear Parents:

This Bible story often is avoided because of its focus on the first murder—surely a violent and frightening image for children. Yet a shift in the focus can become an opportunity for teaching children about God's gifts of grace and forgiveness.

After reading this story, point out that God disapproved of the murder, the act of sin itself. But God did not stop loving Cain. Instead, He placed a mark of mercy, grace, and protection upon Cain. Remind your child that we, too, are marked by the waters of Baptism and that, through Christ's death and resurrection, our sins are forgiven.

Through the power of the Holy Spirit, you can model God's unconditional love to your child. You can say, "I do not like what you did, but I still love you." Then together you can pray a prayer of thanks for God's love, forgiveness, and grace in your lives.

The Editor